ADDRESSING SOCIAL DETERMINANTS OF HEALTH THROUGH INTERSECTORAL ACTIONS:
FIVE PUBLIC POLICY CASES FROM MEXICO

The Series:
The Discussion Paper Series on Social Determinants of Health provides a forum for sharing knowledge on how to tackle the social determinants of health to improve health equity. Papers explore themes related to questions of strategy, governance, tools, and capacity building. They aim to review country experiences with an eye to understanding practice, innovations, and encouraging frank debate on the connections between health and the broader policy environment. Papers are all peer-reviewed.

Background:
The strong causal links between public policies and the social gradient in health were documented in the World Health Organization (WHO) Commission on Social Determinants of Health (CSDH) report. Yet even when health and health equity are seen as important markers of development, expressing benefits of social determinants of health (SDH) interventions in health and health equity terms alone is not always sufficiently persuasive in policy settings where health is not a priority, or when trade-offs need to be made. Previous research has shown that increased attention on policies across sectors that improve health and health equity requires better preparation with regards to knowledge on the economic rationales for interventions, as well with regards to how intersectoral policies are developed and implemented. In recognition of the usefulness of intersectoral actions and the prior experience of Mexico, the Mexican Task Force worked with WHO and PAHO as part of a project titled The economics of social determinants of health, to produce case studies of intersectoral policies, including reference to the use of economic rationales in the process, and to provide input to the other project publication - a resource book on the economics of social determinants of health and health inequalities.

Mexico has been recognized for its work on social policies addressing key health determinants related to poverty and poor living conditions, including for programmes like Oportunidades [Opportunities].

The views presented in this report are those of the author and do not represent the decisions, policies or views of the World Health Organization.

Acknowledgments:
The main researchers in the Mexican Task Force were Adolfo Martínez Valle and Alejandro Figueroa-Lara. The principle writer of the paper was Adolfo Martínez Valle. The Task Force also included Diego González, Sofia Leticia Morales and Kira Fortune from PAHO/WHO; Nicole Valentine from WHO; and Guadalupe López de Llergo and Paulina Terrazas from the Secretariat of Health of Mexico. The health authorities and other government, academic and private institutions in Mexico gave valuable inputs through the interviews process. Comments from Carmen de Paz and Lorenzo Rocco on these documents are much appreciated. The researchers would also like to acknowledge with gratitude the discussions with experts, who were assembled by WHO at the Meeting on the Economics of Social Determinants of Health in October 2012.

Diego González coordinated the Mexican Task Force and Nicole Valentine was responsible for overall project coordination.

The Secretariat of Health of Mexico authorized the publication of this research. Any errors are the responsibility of the writers.
Nicole Valentine and Diego González oversaw the review and production processes. Diana Hopkins provided copy-editing support.
Funding for this project was provided in part by the Public Health Agency of Canada (PHAC). The collaboration of the coordinating project team members from PHAC is gratefully acknowledged, in particular, Jane Laishes, James McDonald and Andrea Long.

Suggested citation:
Martinez Valle A. *Addressing social determinants of health through intersectoral work: Five public policy cases from Mexico.* Social Determinants of Health Discussion Paper Series 6 (Case Studies). Geneva, World Health Organization, 2013.

WHO Library Cataloguing-in-Publication Data
Addressing social determinants of health through intersectoral actions: Five public policy cases from Mexico.
(Discussion Paper Series on Social Determinants of Health, 6)

1.Socioeconomic factors. 2.Health care rationing. 3.Health services accessibility. 4.National health programs. 5.Health policy. 6.Mexico. I.Martinez Valle, Adolfo. II.Figueroa-Lara, Alejandro. III.World Health Organization.

ISBN 978 92 4 150531 4 (NLM classification: WA 525)

© World Health Organization 2013
All rights reserved. Publications of the World Health Organization are available on the WHO web site (www.who.int) or can be purchased from WHO Press, World Health Organization, 20 Avenue Appia, 1211 Geneva 27, Switzerland (tel.: +41 22 791 3264; fax: +41 22 791 4857; e-mail: bookorders@who.int).

Requests for permission to reproduce or translate WHO publications –whether for sale or for non-commercial distribution– should be addressed to WHO Press through the WHO web site (www.who.int/about/licensing/copyright_form/en/index.html).

The designations employed and the presentation of the material in this publication do not imply the expression of any opinion whatsoever on the part of the World Health Organization concerning the legal status of any country, territory, city or area or of its authorities, or concerning the delimitation of its frontiers or boundaries. Dotted lines on maps represent approximate border lines for which there may not yet be full agreement.

The mention of specific companies or of certain manufacturers' products does not imply that they are endorsed or recommended by the World Health Organization in preference to others of a similar nature that are not mentioned. Errors and omissions excepted, the names of proprietary products are distinguished by initial capital letters.

All reasonable precautions have been taken by the World Health Organization to verify the information contained in this publication. However, the published material is being distributed without warranty of any kind, either expressed or implied. The responsibility for the interpretation and use of the material lies with the reader. In no event shall the World Health Organization be liable for damages arising from its use.

The named authors alone are responsible for the views expressed in this publication.

Layout by L'IV Com Sàrl, Villars-sous-Yens, Switzerland.
Printed in Switzerland.

Contents

ABBREVIATIONS   3

EXECUTIVE SUMMARY   4

1 INTRODUCTION   6

2 METHODS   8

3 ANALYTICAL FRAMEWORK FOR ASSESSING INTERSECTORAL PUBLIC POLICIES   10

4 ASSESSING THE INTERSECTORAL PUBLIC POLICY DESIGN AND IMPLEMENTATION PROCESS   12

    4.1 Human Development Programme Oportunidades (PDHO)   12
    4.2 Seguro Popular   14
    4.3 Mexican Road Safety Initiative (IMESEVI)   15
    4.4 Programme for the Development of Priority Zones (PDZP)   17
    4.5 National Agreement for Food Health   18

5 OPPORTUNITIES AND CHALLENGES FOR THE ECONOMICS OF SOCIAL DETERMINANTS OF HEALTH   20

    5.1 Knowledge about social determinants of health   20
    5.2 Intersectoral approach   21
    5.3 Leadership of the Ministry of Health   21
    5.4 Evidence for decision-making   22
    5.5 Using economic arguments for intersectoral public policy   23

6 LESSONS FROM MEXICO   25

REFERENCES AND OTHER RESOURCES   26

    References   26
    Other information resources   28

APPENDIX   30

    Appendix 1. Profile of respondents   30
    Appendix 2. Questionnaire   31

FIGURES

Figure 1. Analytical framework to assess intersectoral public policies: A virtuous cycle — 10
Figure 2. Analytical dimensions of public policy intersectoral implementation — 11
Figure 3. Out-of-pocket as the major source of health financing — 14
Figure 4. Overweight and obesity prevalence rates, 2000–2012 — 18

TABLES

Table 1. Mexican public policies selection criteria — 8
Table 2. Examples of 15 years of results from empirical-based evaluation — 13
Table 3. Main results of IMESEVI evaluation — 16
Table 4. Counties (125) with lowest HDI, by state — 17
Table 5. Economic arguments used for setting the social determinants of health agenda — 24

BOXES

Box 1. Impact of road traffic-related accidents on mortality in Mexico — 16

Abbreviations

ANSA	National Agreement for Food Health
CENAPRA	National Center for Injury Prevention
CSDH	WHO Commission on Social Determinants of Health
HDI	Human Development Index
IMESEVI	Mexican Initiative for Road Safety/Mexican Road Safety Initiative
MOH	Ministry of Health of Mexico
PAHO	Pan American Health Organization
PDHO	Human Development Programme – 'Oportunidades'
PDZP	Programme for the Development of Priority Zones
SDH	Social determinants of health

Executive summary

Currently, the Mexican Health Sector is implementing public policies that tackle the social determinants of health (SDH), mainly to reduce health inequities. However, only a few of these policies involve other sectors. Traditionally, the health sector has taken care of health, despite the fact that the burden of disease is mostly related to the conditions in which many people are born, grow, live, work and age. These social determinants, however, go beyond the realm of the health sector. The participation of other public administration sectors is therefore needed to effectively address SDH such as income, housing, drinking water and education, among others.

The World Health Organization (WHO) is thus fostering a Health in All Policies (HiAP) approach to improve population health by addressing the social determinants of health. This policy approach addresses the social factors that influence health, but which reside outside the health system and in policy sectors other than health. This approach builds on earlier practices of intersectoral collaboration and healthy public policy, but focuses on action in the policy sphere in a more systemic manner rather than applied to single health issues.

However, intersectoral policy-making is difficult because it requires setting common goals, delivering integrated responses and providing increased accountability across government agencies. "To harness health and well-being, governments need institutionalized processes which value cross-sector problem solving and address power imbalances. This includes providing the leadership, mandate, incentives, budgetary commitment and sustainable mechanisms that support government agencies to work collaboratively on integrated solutions." (1)

Despite the difficulties associated with intersectoral coordination, Mexico has gained relevant policy-making evidence that a HiAP approach has important positive efficiency, equity and health effects. Based on these experiences, five public policies were selected, which can provide global lessons for designing and implementing intersectoral actions tackling SDH: the Human Development Programme, Oportunidades, the National Health Insurance Programme, Seguro Popular, the Programme for the Development of Priority Zones, the Mexican Road Safety Initiative and the National Agreement for Food Health.

This document presents the main findings of a research project requested by the Pan American Health Organization (PAHO), the WHO and the Ministry of Health of Mexico aimed at analysing certain policy processes of intersectoral approaches in order to identify evidence sustaining the effectiveness of using a SDH approach to design public policies.

Methods

First, key programmes and policies identified were analysed. Preferentially, programmes and policies that explicitly defined intersectoral actions to fulfill their goals were selected. Second, a literature review was conducted based on the following main subjects: papers analysing an intersectoral approach, public policy analysis, economics of public policy, and the 'grey' policy literature. Its main purpose was to design an analytical framework to assess how intersectoral public policies addressing SDH are designed.

Third, semi-structured interviews were conducted to perform a qualitative analysis of the design and implementation process of the public policies selected, as well as their results. Five categories were used to analyse this information: 1) knowledge of the social determinants of health; 2) intersectoral governance; 3) leadership of the health sector; 4) evidence for decision-making; and 5) economic arguments for intersectoral public policy design and implementation.

Lessons from Mexico

Overall, the analysis of the Mexican public policy cases shows that an intersectoral approach to addressing SDH is feasible, but difficult to implement for three main reasons. First, social factors are still not fully recognized as determinants of health by all policy- and decision-makers, including the medically biased health sector. The term, itself, is not well known. Second, shared budgets or at least resource allocation based on common performance have been proposed, but have not been implemented. Thus, they are still pending windows of opportunity for effectively achieving intersectoral alignment.

Finally, overcoming political barriers is needed to improve intersectoral implementation. Political will and leadership is key at the highest level to achieve intersectoral actions addressing SDH. Furthermore, this intersectoral approach is more effective when it is followed from the beginning of the policy-making process, its planning phase.

Findings show that the design of intersectoral public polices has been based on strong empirical evidence. This has helped their incorporation in the agenda for implementation. However, formal and rigorous evaluations have not been conducted except for Oportunidades and Seguro Popular. The more recent public policies analysed in this paper, the Programme for the Development of Priority Zones, the Mexican Road Safety Initiative, and the National Agreement for Healthy Food have not been fully implemented and evaluated. While the need to evaluate arises, budgets tend to be targeted more often to implementing projects than to measuring their impact on health and other determinants.

Economic arguments such as the return on investment in recreational spaces for physical activities, estimating the cost-effectiveness of preventive measures, or measuring the financial protection effects of public insurance schemes such as Seguro Popular are necessary, but not sufficient to convince decision-makers both within and outside the health sector to design and implement public policies tackling SDH. Other arguments such as empirical evidence of health benefits or the ethical value of health itself are also useful for pushing these public policies onto the agenda, particularly if there is very little information in economic or monetary terms to both assess and support these types of policies.

1 Introduction

Currently, the Mexican Health Sector is implementing public policies that tackle the social determinants of health[1] (SDH), mainly to reduce health inequities[2]. However, only a few of these policies involve other sectors. Traditionally, the health sector has taken care of health, despite the fact that the burden of disease is mostly related to the conditions in which many people are born, grow, live, work and age. These social determinants, however, go beyond the realm of the health sector. The participation of other public administration sectors is therefore needed to effectively address SDH such as income, housing, drinking water and education, among others.

The World Health Organization (WHO) is thus fostering a Health in All Policies (HiAP) approach to improve population health. This policy principle addresses the social factors that influence health, but which reside outside the health system and in policy sectors other than health. This approach builds on earlier practices of intersectoral collaboration and health public policy, but focuses on action in the policy sphere in a more systemic manner rather than applied to single health issues *(1)*.

However, intersectoral policy-making is difficult because it requires setting common goals, delivering integrated responses and providing increased accountability across government agencies. "To harness health and well-being, governments need institutionalized processes which value cross-sector problem solving and address power imbalances. This includes providing the leadership, mandate, incentives, budgetary commitment and sustainable mechanisms that support government agencies to work collaboratively on integrated solutions." *(1)*

Despite these difficulties for intersectoral coordination, Mexico provides relevant policy-making evidence that this systemic HiAP approach[3] has important positive efficiency, equity and health effects. Two of the most important recent intersectoral public policies addressing SDH in Mexico are the 15-year-old Human Development Programme named Oportunidades (PDHO), a conditional cash transfer programme, that requires the participation of three social policy sectors: social development, health and education, and the more recent one, the so-called Seguro Popular de Salud (SPS), a national insurance scheme designed and implemented since 2002 to financially protect the income of the population not covered by social insurance. The experience of PDHO has allowed the effectiveness of joint actions of the three participating sectors to be assessed to improve the extreme poverty conditions in which nearly a quarter of the total population in Mexico has been living for the past two decades. PDHO has systematically shown relevant direct impacts on health outcomes and on their social determinants since its implementation *(4)*.

---

1 Social determinants are "those factors or mechanisms through which social conditions influence health". In other words, "it is the way in which people live and work that has an effect on health" *(2)*.

2 Inequity is the presence of systematic and potentially addressable differences among socially, economically or geographically defined people *(3)*.

3 A "Health in All Policies" approach is one in which the actions are taken in a coordinated manner to improve the impact or accountability of public policies across sectors on population health, health equity, health-related human rights and health systems. It highlights the important links between health and broader economic and social goals in modern societies, and considers the effects of policies on social determinants as well as the beneficial impact of improvements in health on the goals of other sectors. It assists leaders and policy-makers to integrate considerations of health, well-being and equity during the development, implementation and evaluation of policies and services.

More recently, the Seguro Popular experience has shown that the health sector can be effective in developing public policies that address social determinants such as income *(5)*. By seeking to expand health insurance to the uninsured population, which was mostly the low-income Mexican families, Seguro Popular had a positive impact on the equity of public-health expenditure *(5,6)*. It reduced both the inequities in resource allocation between the insured and the uninsured populations, as well as among states.

Based on these experiences, WHO selected Mexico as a case study to provide global lessons for designing and implementing intersectoral actions to tackle SDH. This document presents the main findings of a research project requested by the Pan American Health Organization (PAHO), the World Health Organization and the Ministry of Health of Mexico (MOH) aimed at identifying feasible intersectoral strategies that effectively address SDH.

To achieve this, this document first defines an analytical framework, based on a systematic literature review, to assess how these types of policies were designed and implemented and their effects both on the SDH and health itself. Second, it presents the main findings of in-depth interviews with key actors participating in the design and implementation of these policies. Finally, it incorporates the key findings and proposals of the position paper that explored the economic arguments *(7,8,9,10)* used to justify intersectoral public policies addressing SDH in Mexico. Key objectives were to:

1. analyse the policy process of intersectoral approaches in order to identify evidence sustaining the effectiveness of using a SDH approach to design public policies;
2. design an analytical framework to assess the effectiveness of intersectoral and sectoral public policies tackling SDH in Mexico;
3. identify good practices, effective strategies (including economic arguments) and governance structures that trigger intersectoral action on SDH to reduce health inequities;
4. recommend strategies to underpin the leadership of the MOH on conducting an intersectoral approach to address SDH;
5. identify lessons from Mexico to use when designing and implementing intersectoral actions to tackle SDH in other countries.

2 Methods

First, key programmes and policies identified by the Mexican SDH Task Force will be analysed[1]. Preferentially, programmes and policies that explicitly defined intersectoral actions[2] to fulfill their goals were selected. Also, public policies designed by the health sector aiming to tackle SDH will be analysed. This initial research phase was based on a systematic review of published official documents related to federal public policies[3] that address SDH with an intersectoral approach.

Table 1 shows the selection criteria of the five programmes or policies analysed identifyng explictly an addressable SDH, using economic arguments, as well as having evidence-based policy design and evaluation results. The table also shows their year of implementation.

Second, a literature review (12) was conducted based on the following main subjects: papers analysing an intersectoral approach, public policy analysis, economics of public policy, and the 'grey' policy literature. Its main purpose was to design an analytical framework to assess how intersectoral public policies are addressing SDH are designed. This framework will also help to analyse the implementation process of the public policies selected above in order to find evidence that justifies using a SDH approach to design and implement public policies.

---

1 The main researchers in the Mexican Task Force created for this project were Adolfo Martínez Valle and Alejandro Figueroa. The Task Force also included Diego González, Sofía Leticia Morales and Kira Fortune from PAHO/WHO; Nicole Valentine from WHO; and Guadalupe López de Llergo and Paulina Terrazas from the Secretariat of Health of Mexico.
2 Intersectoral actions are defined here as policies conducted by other sectors in collaboration with the health sector to achieve specific health goals or to explicitly address SDH. See Health Equity Through Intersectoral Action (11).
3 For the purposes of this research project, only federal programmes or public policies will be analysed.

Table 1. Mexican public policies selection criteria

Public Policy	Key SDH	Economic arguments	Evidence-based design	Evaluation results	Year
Oportunidades	Poverty	Yes	Yes	Yes	1997
Seguro Popular	Income	Yes	Yes	Yes	2002
Priority Zones for Social Development	Underdevelopment	Yes	Yes	No	2003
Mexican Road Safety Initiative	Education	Yes	Yes	Yes	2008
National Agreement for Food Health	Education	Yes	Yes	No	2010

Third, semi-structured interviews[4] were conducted to perform a qualitative analysis of the design and implementation process of the public policies selected, as well as their results. The following five analytical categories were defined:
- knowledge of the social determinants of health
- intersectoral governance
- leadership of the health sector
- evidence for decision-making
- economic arguments for intersectoral public policy design and implementation.

Although 30 interviews were originally scheduled, only 13 were completed due to time constraints[5].

The profile of the key informants was both senior researchers and policy-makers with at least 10 years in the field. More specifically, these interviews were made to identify policy lessons and windows of opportunity, as well as the obstacles faced in implementing intersectoral actions to address SDH.

Finally, some policy lessons will be drawn from this framework for designing and implementing public policies both in Mexico and other countries.

---
4 To review the contents of the questionnaire see Appendix 2 of this document. It is based on questions formulated for similar research purposes in other studies made by DETERMINE, a consortium for action on SDH from the European Union.
5 A similar project conducted in Europe managed to make nearly 30 interviews, but within a much longer time frame and involving more than 15 researchers.

3 Analytical framework for assessing intersectoral public policies

The framework proposed is based on a literature review of three general categories: intersectoral approaches, public policies addressing the SDH, and public policy analysis *(12,13,14,15,16,17)*. It suggests, as Figure 1 shows, that public policy design and implementation are essential components of a continuous virtuous cycle.

From the beginning, the design of public policies should be based on empirical evidence showing their feasibility in addressing a public issue. This evidence may include either a diagnosis of a situation, a best practice to tackle a similar public health problem, or economic arguments such as the cost-effectiveness of implementing a healthy public policy.

Figure 1. Analytical framework to assess intersectoral public policies: A virtuous cycle

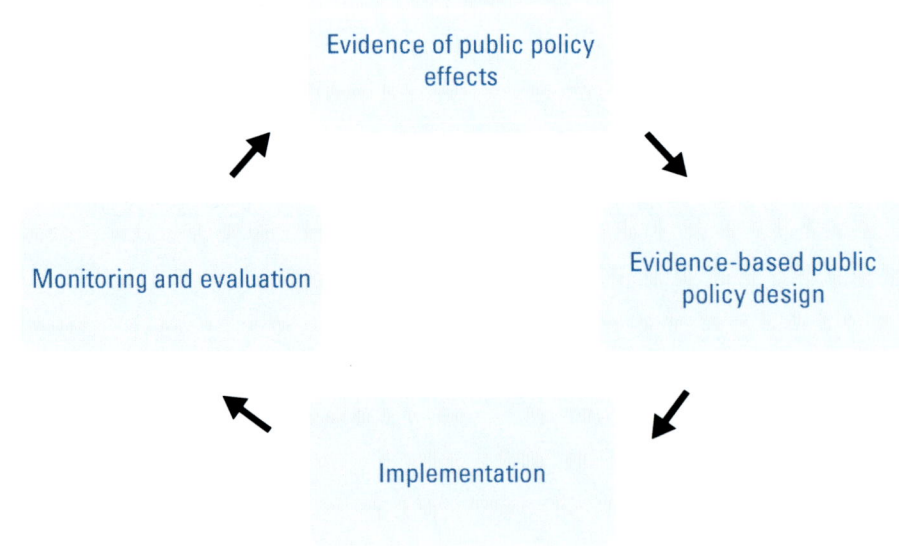

The second step is the evidence-based design itself, followed by implementation. To analyse the implementation process of intersectoral public policies more thoroughly, Figure 2 suggests three dimensions: shared political vision; sectorial alignment; and public policy results.

Sharing a vision is key to successfully implementing an intersectoral public policy. Three characteristics of this first component are essential. First, the agenda for intersectoral action needs to be jointly defined by all or most of the participating governmental agencies and nongovernmental organizations. Second, a legal mandate is necessary to enforce such a common agenda. Finally, the MOH should effectively lead it.

All participating government agencies should align their goals by defining common objectives, maximizing budgets, and monitoring their joint performance using shared indicators. Finally, public policy should be designed and implemented based on the best empirical evidence available on the effects of similar public policies on SDH, the synergistic effect of intersectoral policies, as well as economic evidence that support its investment.

The cycle is completed at the last phase when the monitoring and evaluation results provide enough evidence for policy-makers to decide whether they keep implementing the public policy as originally designed or scale it up or improve it if the results are positive, or discard it if it produces undesirable or unsatisfactory results. Intersectoral public policies addressing SDH are quantitatively evaluated, either by measuring their effectiveness in achieving defined goals such as improving health, by evaluating their impact in the time frame defined in terms of equity, or by assessing them with an economic perspective such as cost-effectiveness or cost-benefit analysis.

Figure 2. Analytical dimensions of public policy intersectoral implementation

4 Assessing the intersectoral public policy design and implementation process

Five intersectoral public policies addressing SDH were selected for analysis: Oportunidades, Seguro Popular, the Program for the Development of Priority Zones for Social Development, the Mexican Road Safety Initiative and the National Agreement for Food Health. All of them share the criteria shown in Table 1. Their differences lie in their years of implementation and their degree of success in addressing the social determinants for which they were designed. Each of them will be assessed using the analytical framework defined previously and emphasizing the dimensions of public policy intersectoral action identified above to analyse the implementation process.

4.1 Human Development Programme Oportunidades (PDHO)

Oportunidades is a conditional cash transfer programme, created in 1997, to help households, in the long run, break out of a vicious cycle whereby poverty is transmitted from one generation to another. To achieve this, it provides financial incentives through cash transfers to promote child health, nutrition and schooling.

Oportunidades was originally designed based on strong empirical evidence. Nearly two decades before this, a growing body of scientific literature both from the social and the health sciences led to a more comprehensive understanding of poverty determinants (18). This research emphasized the links between food intake, nutrition, health and education, suggesting that an integrated rather than an isolated approach to delivering services could be more effective and efficient in tackling the nutritional, health, and educational needs of the poor. This knowledge was systematically incorporated into the design of Oportunidades, which at the time was called Progresa[1]. Furthermore, there was some agreement, particularly from officials in the Finance Ministry that the food subsidies in place at that time were inadequate to protect the poor, mainly because a large share of the benefits were received by the non-poor and targeted programmes had very limited coverage in rural areas (18).

The accumulated empirical evidence and economic arguments helped to gradually persuade the members of the Cabinet to make adjustments to the existing food subsidy and related poverty programmes that led to the design of Progresa 15 years ago (18). However, building a shared political vision was difficult to achieve. Presidential leadership was essential to the implementation of the programme. An initiative from the Executive Branch legally mandated Progresa in 1997[2].

Since then, the implementation of Oportunidades has involved intersectoral participation of the Ministry of Social Development (SEDESOL), the Ministry of Health, the Ministry of Education (SEP), and the Ministry of Finance (SHCP). This required sectoral alignment to effectively coordinate the activities of the implementing agencies and ministries within the Executive Branch.

---

1 Progresa stands for Programa de Educación, Salud y Alimentación (Education, Health, and Food Programme).
2 This decree was issued on August 8, 1997 when the National Coordination Unit of Progresa, the government agency in charge of the programme was created as part of the Ministry of Social Development.

Common goals were set for all of them. Budgets were reallocated to each of them in order to achieve such goals and shared performance indicators were designed. All of these are published yearly in the so-called 'operational rules' and are regularly monitored by Congress and the SHCP. Also, to monitor these goals and indicators, a Technical Committee was created, which meets regularly to oversee progress and evaluate the programme with the participation of all the agencies and ministries involved.

Finally, evaluation played a key role in the continuity of the programme. Since the beginning, Oportunidades has been systematically evaluated by both international and national independent academic researchers, who have measured its effects, as well as identified windows of opportunity to improve its design. Table 2 summarizes the main evaluation results of this 15-year-old programme.

Although Oportunidades has achieved important reductions in maternal and infant mortality, as well as improving nutritional conditions in families living in extreme poverty, it faces important challenges in the long run: achieving the better education, nutrition and health outcomes that contribute to overcoming the living conditions of extreme poverty; and linking them to economic policies that allow beneficiaires to gradually join the labour force and improve their life-time income.

To achieve such outcomes, improving the quality of both health and education services is essential. In education, for example, intersectoral alignment is needed to overcome high drop-out rates at the middle-school level, where quality is worst and the opportunity costs of not working are high among adolescents. A new strategy that is now being evaluated is to provide early education to improve school achievement at higher grades. Sound empirical evidence has shown that the first five years are crucial in developing physical, linguistic, cognitive, and socio-emotional skills that will help them to fully benefit from further opportunities in the education and health sectors, as well as become fully productive members of society. Furthermore, early childhood development is a cost-effective strategy in making children healthier, and helping them to perform better in school, engage in less risky activities, and become more productive adults *(20)*.

Table 2. Examples of 15 years of results from empirical-based evaluation

Effects			
Health	Higher primary care, both preventive and curative, in rural (35%) and urban areas (26%).	Maternal mortality was reduced by 11%, while infant mortality was reduced by 2%, both at the national level.	Nearly a 20% reduction in days ill in 0–5-year-old children in rural areas.
Nutrition	Height increased 1.42 cm in children younger than 2 years old in urban areas.	–	–
Education	1-year higher schooling among 15–19 year olds receiving scholarships for 10 years in rural areas, compared to a 0.6-year higher among those receiving scholarships during a 6-year period.	Higher enrolment in middle-school (23%) of Oportunidades scholars compared to non-Oportunidades scholars.	Lower drop-out rates (23%) among 16–19 year-olds in urban areas.

– = Not determined.
Source: *(19)*.

4.2 Seguro Popular[3]

Seguro Popular is a voluntary public insurance scheme seeking to reduce the proportion of household spending from out-of-pocket payments, to lower the prevalence of household castastrophic expenditures, and increase access to insurance coverage. Its target population is families not covered by social security.

Furthermore, Seguro Popular was designed in 2001 to address five economic issues of the health system *(21)*:

1. the low level of overall spending;
2. the reliance on out-of-pocket spending as the major source of health financing;
3. inequity in resource allocation between insured and uninsured, and among states;
4. inequitable contribution of resources by states; and
5. under-investment in infrastructure.

Figure 3 shows convincing empirical evidence for advancing Seguro Popular as an instrument to address the most regressive way of financing health care: more than half of the total expenditure in Mexico was out-of-pocket direct payments[4].

Although the most important goal of Seguro Popular was to achieve effective coverage, and ultimately improve health, these economic arguments were originally used before implementation to convince the main financial decision-makers in Mexico that more resources were needed to achieve a more equitable and universal national health system.

Both international and national studies provided empirical evidence that supported this economic approach. The WHO framework for health-system performance assessment emphasized fairness of financing as one of the intrinsic goals of health systems. As a result of its high percentage of out-of-pocket spending, Mexico appeared as a poor perfomer on the international comparative analysis of this indicator. This led to a detailed country-level analysis, based on the 2000 National Income and Expenditure Survey that showed that castastrophic expenditures were concentrated in poor and uninsured households *(23)*.

---

3 Although Seguro Popular is not an intersectoral public policy, except for the interactions between the Ministry of Health and the Ministry of Finance, it was selected for the Mexican case because it shares the three dimensions defined in the analytical framework: shared political vision, sectoral alignment, and evidence-based policy-making.

4 This source of financing represented a higher proportion of income in poorer households than in richer ones.

Figure 3. Out-of-pocket as the major source of health financing

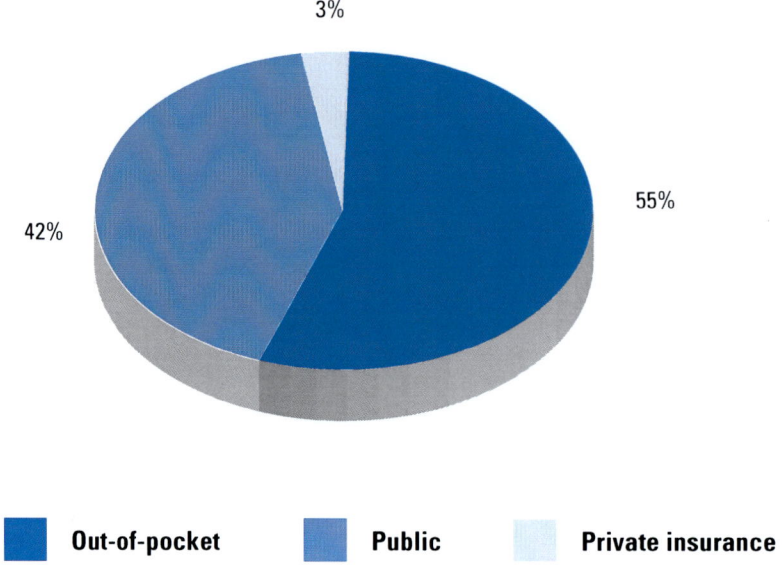

Source: *(22)*.

Furthermore, a pilot study was conducted in 2001 and evaluated in 2002, using a National Health Insurance Survey and focus groups to assess the needs and expectations of the target population of Seguro Popular. Among the key findings was the high willingness to affiliate to such a voluntary health-insurance scheme, especially if it provided care and medicines for chronic illness. Also, it was found that people were willing to pay for a premium if coverage proved to be effective. These main findings enabled the programme to gradually scale the scheme up from 60 000 affiliated families in five states to more than 600 000 in 2003 when the legal mandate for Seguro Popular was achieved with the reform to the General Health Law *(24)*.

Thus, health policy-makers extended their focus to include economic arguments that proved to have a great effect on health-care provision and on poverty in Mexican households *(23)*. This helped the Ministry of Health to share the same political vision with the Ministry of Finance, as well as align resources to common goals and indicators.

The National Health Programme, 2007–2012[5], formulated two strategic goals to avoid impoverishment for health reasons: (i) reduce the share of out-of-pocket expenditure from total health spending to 44 per cent; and (ii) reduce the proportion of households that face catastrophic health expenditures by 10 per cent.

Regarding the first goal, out-of-pocket expenditure was reduced from 51.7 per cent in 2004 to 47.1 per cent in 2010, according to the more recent available evidence *(25)*. The second goal was achieved when the proportion of households that face catastrophic health expenditures fell from 3.6 per cent to 2.8 per cent, which represents a 20.6 per cent reduction *(25)*.

Seguro Popular has provided financial protection for its targeted population. These achievements, however, pose additional challenges in the long run. Once Seguro Popular reaches universal affiliation of its targeted population, it still needs to strengthen the supply of health services in order to achieve effective coverage.

---

5 http://www.preventionweb.net/files/11938_PlanNacionaldeSP.pdf (accessed 25 March 2013).

4.3 Mexican Road Safety Initiative (IMESEVI)

IMESEVI is an intersectoral strategy headed by the Ministry of Health with the joint participation of the Ministry of Communicactions and Transportation and the Ministry of Public Security. It seeks to reduce road injuries, disability and deaths, by promoting road safety, preventing injuries, and improving care for the injured population *(26)*. It started in 2008 after a study gathered evidence showing that the isolated efforts of multiple institutions and agencies were not going to be able to effectively address this multisectoral public health problem.

Coordination was found to be essential to achieve the common goals of reducing road injuries and their serious consequences on health. Besides these shared objetives, sectoral alignment was possible due to the financial support of the Bloomberg Foundation and the technical support of PAHO and WHO.

For many years, few resources for preventing injuries had been allocated to the Ministry of Health and little could be achieved. However, with the leadership of the National Center for Injury Prevention (CENAPRA), the agency within the Ministry of Health in charge of these issues, and international support from the Bloomberg Foundation, this initative, which started as a pilot study, soon became the National Strategy for Road Safety. WHO's call for the Decade for Action for Road Safety also helped to support this initiative.

Besides this intersectoral approach to reducing road traffic injuries, sound empirical evidence was key to advancing this initiative and identifying specific policy solutions. According to WHO, nearly half of the total road-traffic deaths worldwide are related to the three most vulnerable road users: pedestrians, bicyclists, and motorcyclists. In Mexico, these users represent approximately 60 per cent of total road-traffic deaths *(27)*. Box 1 shows the impact of road-traffic accidents on mortality in the past decade.

IMESEVI fosters intersectoral actions to reduce driving under the influence of alcohol and to

Box 1. Impact of road traffic-related accidents on mortality in Mexico

- Between 1999 and 2010, 185 000 people died from road traffic-related injuries.
- These numbers are probably 30 per cent higher due to the fact that data collection on road safety is not registered or is mis-classified.
- Pedestrians are the most vulnerable road-user group, representing almost half of the deaths from road traffic-related injuries.
- The mortality rate of motorcycle users increased 332 per cent between 1999 and 2009.

Source: *(27)*.

enforce speeding limits, promote the use of seat belts and child seats for cars, and the use of helmets for motorcyclists. Table 3 shows the positive effects of four key road safety instruments promoted by IMESEVI.

Table 3. Main results of IMESEVI evaluation

Policy instrument	Target population	Effect
Belt seats	Everybody	12% higher use
Child seats	>5-year-old	48% higher use
Belts seats	Taxi users	28% higher use
Child seats	Family vans	56% higher use

Source: *(28)*.

These findings have provided empirical evidence that joint actions to enforce the use of safety instruments with an adequate communication strategy yield important results in preventing injuries. Furthermore, empirical evidence, particularly on the economic impact of injuries was particularly convincing for decision-makers when allocating resources. Together, road traffic-related injuries, disabilities and deaths account for nearly US$ 1 billion annually in Mexico *(29)*.

An agreement signed by the Ministry of Health and the Ministry of Communications and Transportation in 2011, legally mandated IMESEVI, with the participation of both state and local governments. However, a formal committment from the Federal Police is lacking. This hinders effective enforcement of road traffic laws.

Sectoral alignment was achieved through shared commons goals to reduce traffic-related deaths by 50 per cent, as well as diminishing injuries and disabilities *(30)*. However, these indicators are only measured at the national level. Indicators are lacking for both state and local governments. Furthermore, budgets have not been fully estimated, so it is not clear how much is needed to achieve these common goals.

In sum, IMESEVI is an intersectoral policy that addresses socially determined road-injury risks through safe road promotion strategies. It was designed and implemented based on empirical evidence. The great economic burden of injuries was a very convincing argument for including this initiative in the policy agenda.

4.4 Programme for the Development of Priority Zones (PDZP)[6]

This programme was designed in 2003 to articulate intersectoral actions[7] and address underdevelopment in the 125 counties with the lowest Human Development Index (HDI)[8]. Table 4 shows how are these counties are distributed by state as well as their average HDI.

Table 4. Counties (125) with lowest HDI, by state

States	Counties	HDI
Chiapas	20	0.49
Durango	1	0.52
Guerrero	21	0.45
Nayarit	1	0.49
Oaxaca	58	0.51
Puebla	9	0.55
Veracruz	15	0.52
TOTAL	125	0.50

Source: *(31)*.

This intersectoral policy was basically a coordination strategy for all Federal Government agencies that sought to articulate actions, together with state and local authorities, to address underdevelopment, which has an important impact on health. An important share of the burden of disease in these deprived regions is still attributable to infectious diseases, malnutrition and reproductive health issues, such as maternal mortality. The risk of dying from an infectious disease is twice as likely as in the rest of the country and, for maternal causes, it is three times higher than the Mexican average. Life expectancy is 51 years old for women and 49 for men, compared with the national averages of 78 and 73, respectively *(32)*.

Despite the fact that this evidence led to the design of a well-informed intersectoral public policy, implementation was not very successful because there was no shared political vision among all participating government agencies nor was sectoral alignment fully achieved. Regarding the first dimension, the Ministry of Social Development, who coordinated the intersectoral actions, could not exercise effective leadership. Furthermore, even though a common agenda was set, a legal mandate was lacking. Many ministries and government agencies participated: the ministries of health, education and communications and transportation, as well as the National Water Commission and the National Commission for the Development of Indigenous People, among others.

Sectoral alignment was difficult because common goals were not defined, budgets were not jointly allocated and indicators were not shared. However, monitoring of this programme was effective in the beginning. All Federal Government agencies initally recognized the importance of joint actions to improve living conditions of the most underdeveloped regions of Mexico.

Despite these initial efforts, the indicators used to monitor the programme were incomplete, not useful, and more importantly were not shared. Furthermore, an evaluation strategy was not formally designed.

Thus, an intersectoral opportunity to address several social determinants of health in the most deprived counties in Mexico was lost due to the lack of both shared political vision and effective sectoral alignment.

---

[6] Programa de Desarrollo de Zonas Prioritarias.
[7] These actions address six dimensions of human development: health, education, housing, income, social infrastructure, and ecological sustainability.
[8] The HDI was designed by the United Nations Development Programme. It is a three-component indicator: life expectancy, schooling and living standards (income statistics). Its values range from 0 to 1, where 1 equals full development and 0 no development.

4.5 National Agreement for Food Health

Strong empirical evidence of overweight and obesity in Mexico, and its economic consequences made an important contribution in establishing a shared political vision for this serious public health problem within the Federal Government. Figure 4 shows that the prevalence of overweight has not been reduced in the past decade and obesity has increased in the same period, reaching nearly 27 per cent in 2012.

The evidence on economic impact was even more dramatic in policy terms. The estimated direct cost of medical care attributable to overweight and obesity increased 61 per cent from 26 283 million pesos in 2000 to approximately 42 246 million pesos in 2008. This represents 33 per cent of the total medical budget available for that year. In 2008, the cost for 2017 was estimated at 77 919 million pesos *(33)*. On the other hand, the estimated indirect costs due to the productivity loss of premature death attributable to overweight and obesity has increased at an annual rate of 13.5 per cent. Together, both indirect and direct costs are estimated to increase to more than 150 million pesos by the year 2017.

The economic burden that these costs represent for the sustainability of the public health-care system has helped the MOH to convince other sectors, particularly the Ministry of Finance, that intersectoral actions are urgently needed to address this public health problem. The following 10 objectives were defined:

❶ promote physical activity in schools, at work, and in the community and recreational settings with the collaboration of the public, private and social sectors;
❷ increase availability, accessibility and consumption of safe drinking water;
❸ reduce the sugar and fat content in drinks;
❹ increase daily consumption of healthy food, such as fruits and vegetables by increasing its accessibility and by demostrating its positive effects;
❺ improve decision-making on an adequate diet by improving food labelling and fostering healthy food consumption;
❻ promote exclusive breast feeding for the first six months and foster adequate feeding from that age on;
❼ reduce consumption of food high in sugar and other sweeteners by increasing availability and accessibility of food low in sugar;

Figure 4. Overweight and obesity prevalence rates, 2000–2012

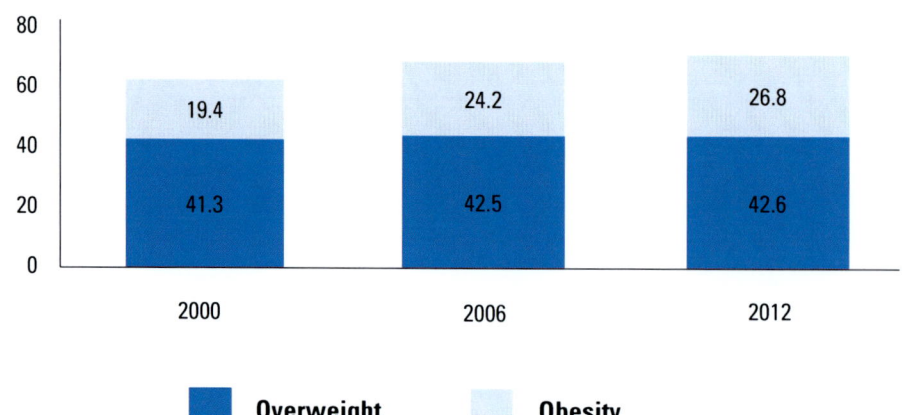

Source: *(32)*.

8. diminish daily consumption of saturated fat in regular diet and minimize consumption of transfat products of industrial origin;
9. guide consumers on optimal serving sizes for homemade meals as well as restaurant menus and food stands;
10. diminish daily consumption of sodium by reducing the quantity of added sodium, and increasing the availability and accessibility of products low in sodium or without sodium.

The National Agreement for Food Health (ANSA)[9] began its intersectoral implementation in 2010 with the signature of 15 public government agencies and five business groups. Shortly afterwards, the Ministry of Education presented its programme, which included as one of its main strategies general guidelines for food and beverage consumption in every elementary and middle school across the country[10]. This legal mandate provided the starting point for intersectoral action in schools, where the potential for obtaining results in addressing overweight and obesity is higher.

Targeting the school-aged population helped to establish a common agenda between the Ministry of Health and the Ministry of Education. Finding a common policy ground is useful for sharing a political vision and fostering sectoral alignment. This intersectoral synergy could then produce more effective results in preventing and controlling obesity and overweight. Specific indicators have been defined to measure these results, but currently there is no evidence available to account for its effects. There is, however, a recent study that evaluates the implementation process of the previously mentioned school guidelines for food and beverage consumption by identifying the factors that support and hinder their enforcement (34). However, a rigorous evaluation of this public policy is still lacking.

In conclusion, this intersectoral public policy was well informed by gathering strong empirical evidence of both the magnitude and the economic consequences of the public health issue it addressed. However, it is too early to assess whether this policy has been successful because it has not been fully implemented and its effects have not been measured yet.

---

[9] Acuerdo Nacional de Salud Alimentaria.
[10] These guidelines were officially published on August 23rd after a broad-based process of public consultation.

5 Opportunities and challenges for the economics of social determinants of health

Using evidence from the previous analysis and the content of the interviews of key decision-makers and researchers, each policy will be assessed, examining several influencing factors, which have been grouped for analytical purposes into five categories:
- knowledge of the social determinants of health
- intersectoral governance
- leadership from the Ministry of Health
- evidence for decision-making
- acceptability of using economic arguments for intersectoral public policy.

5.1 Knowledge about social determinants of health

Overall, evidence from the interviews indicated that social determinants are well identified. The role of social factors such as income, education and employment are recognized. However, they are seldom defined as determinants of health. Furthermore, most respondents acknowledge that public policies in Mexico address them, but not necessarily to impact health or reduce health inequalities. Therefore, in order to advance the agenda to tackle SDH, an important window of opportunity is to foster greater awareness among key decision- and policy-makers of how these social factors influence health. As an important public health decision-maker stated:

Health is an issue that should be addressed from a multisectoral perspective…if this is not well understood, it will be very difficult to tackle most causes of health problems, except maybe for genetic or biologically determined factors.

Except for the Ministry of Social Development, who is in charge of the Oportunidades programme, outside of the health sector, general knowledge about SDH is neither recognized nor given value in terms of the health outcomes of their policies. Non-health intersectoral policy actors need to become aware that they have the organizational space, the resources and even a mandate to define appropriate action to address SDH.

The most important challenge, however, lies in the health sector itself. Historically, the MOH and the social security institutions that provide public health care have adopted a medical-care approach to address population health. Most of the top decision-makers in the health sector have been physicians that lack a public health background, preventing them from fully understanding social factors such as income, education, housing or transportation as determinants of health.

Most respondents acknowledged that this knowledge gap requires investment in the training of policy-makers from both within and outside the health sector, especially legislators who besides the Federal Government have the power to decide how resources are allocated between the multiple public programmes and policies in Mexico. They emphasized, however, the training of medical and health professionals, who should assume a leadership role in fostering an intersectoral approach for addressing SDH.

5.2 Intersectoral approach

Findings show that intersectoral actions are difficult to monitor within the Mexican Federal Government, but that its implementation is feasible. Several instruments and mechanisms have been identified to effectively conduct an intersectoral approach. First, formal coordinating bodies or committees, such as permanent intersectoral task force groups have been helpful in articulating actions across sectors. For example, the Technical Committee of Oportunidades summons middle-level officials from the ministries of social development, health, education, finance and transparency to attend regular meetings where decisions are made regarding changes to the operational rules of the programme; performance is assessed using key indicators; and where evaluation results are reviewed.

Legal mandates are also fundamental in articulating actions among participating government agencies. All of the policy cases reviewed here had a legal mandate, except for PDZP, which was unable to share a political vision or establish an effective intersectoral alignment.

Besides these institutional and legal mechanisms, economic incentives represent a window of opportunity to better align intersectoral actions. Decision-maker respondents shared the view that allocating specific resources to achieve common goals would create the positive incentives needed to create a synergistic effect. Moreover, payment should be based on performance. Currently, the Ministry of Finance has produced the necessary rules, but has not yet managed to fully enforce them. The main challenge is the effective implementation of monitoring and accountability mechanisms to sustain such an approach.

Both top-down and bottom-up strategies seem effective in encouraging intersectoral actions. Political will and decision-making at the highest level was more decisive in giving these public policies high priority on the political agenda. All of the intersectoral public policies analysed here had support from the ministers of the sectors involved and, apart from IMESEVI, all received backing from the President.

Bottom-up strategies were also helpful. The participation of state and local governments played an important role in enhancing the feasibility of implementing Oportunidades and Seguro Popular. The failed PDZP managed to articulate more effective intersectoral actions at the county level from the initiatives of the local authorities rather than from the representatives of the multiple Federal Government agencies. Finally, shared goals are key to effectively align all actors. A policy-maker from the Ministry of Social Development stressed its importance:

To pursue the same goals, each sector has to recognize that its actions contribute to the achievement of such goals.

It was more difficult to identify indicators to measure such goals and, even if an indicator was agreed upon, reliable information was not usually available to measure it.

5.3 Leadership of the Ministry of Health

While the National Development Plan and the National Health Sector Programme set overall government goals for supporting the economic case, evidence from the interviews suggests that leadership must come from within the MOH. Two strong arguments have been made. First, health is a 'politically correct' issue, except maybe when a public policy such as ANSA threatens the vested interests of industries commercializing food high in sugar, salt and fat. But within the government, it is very rare that a health issue faces opposition.

Health in itself is considered to be good because it contributes to an individual's well-being, happiness or satisfaction. As a top policy-maker from the Ministry of Social Development stated:

> *What ultimately allowed us to sit at the same table, to commit to specific action, such as investing in sewage and improving housing conditions as well as to agree on a common goal was an improvement in health.*

Also, knowledge of the factors that have an impact on health is more likely to be acknowledged within the health sector. It is in the interests of the health sector itself that other government agencies become aware of the positive effects that fighting poverty, improving housing conditions and maintaining safe roads have on health.

The challenge lies in how to exercise this leadership among different sectors. First of all, a common and clear language delivered by the health sector and understood by all stakeholders, including the private sector is needed. Respondents from the interviews suggested that meaningful arguments to support health should be clearer and be presented in language that speaks to policy-makers across a range of sectors, particularly government agencies of social development and education.

Second, identifying health policy areas of mutual interest with other sectors is helpful for intersectoral alignment. Public elementary schools were the most feasible policy space where banning unhealthy food for school-aged children's consumption could have a significant impact in the long run. The Ministry of Health understood that, but more importantly the Ministry of Education also acknowledged the potential effects of preventing obesity and overweight in school-aged children.

5.4 Evidence for decision-making

Usually, good evidence is used for designing intersectoral public policies in Mexico, including economic arguments. The evidence focuses either on the benefits for health or the cost effectiveness of implementing a preventive public policy such as IMESEVI or ANSA rather than paying later for the consequences of not preventing road-related injuries or an obesegenic environment. Moreover, economic analysis is often provided in broad terms. Most information does not go into detail about the projected cost-benefits or cost-efficiency in monetary terms. One important challenge, according to one of the senior researchers interviewed was the following:

> *The main sources of good and reliable health information usually do not gather cost and monetary information, while good and reliable information on costs and monetary terms is not collected for health monitoring purposes.*

According to the available evidence, once implemented, not all public policies are rigorously evaluated, except for Oportunidades. Although by law, every health-related policy should undergo some form of evaluation, existing evaluation guidelines are not always followed because they are difficult to effectively enforce.

Moreover, while it is recommended that health-related policies should be subject to regular and rigorous evaluation before, during and after implementation, there appears to be a lack of economic assessments in evaluations actually completed. Except for Seguro Popular and Oportunidades, it is less common to measure economic impact.

Both the analysis and the interviews also suggest that international evidence and support from WHO are important when seeking support from difficult stakeholders such as industries producing food high in sugar, salt and fat. Signing the ANSA agreement would not have been feasible without the call from WHO to reduce obesity, and the available empirical evidence to support it. Similar backing was important for incorporating the prevention of road-traffic injuries into the agenda of the Ministry of Health with the IMESEVI initiative.

5.5 Using economic arguments for intersectoral public policy

Existing empirical evidence suggested almost 12 years ago that health is responsible for approximately a third of its potential economic growth using data from 1970–1995 *(35)*. The Mexican Commission on Macroeconomics and Health was created in 2002, following the example of the WHO Commission on Macroeconomics and Health, to further assess the relationship between health investment and economic development, especially in reducing poverty and inequities.

The Mexican Commission itself was a result of an intersectoral initiative between the Ministry of Health and the Ministry of Finance. Overall, the Mexican Commission found that there are strong economic arguments for investing in health at the population level because it has the potential to foster economic growth and reduce poverty through social protection schemes such as Seguro Popular. It can also diminish social inequities by investing in social capital such as by improving nutrition at an early age to achieve higher schooling levels, especially among the poor *(36)*. This was probably the first institutional effort in Mexico to explicitly use economic arguments to justify a higher investment in health, which led to the design and implementation of Seguro Popular.

The acceptability of using economic arguments to support action on SDH received mixed responses from interviewees. Some of them, particularly those within the health sector, suggested that economic arguments were not routinely used because of a lack of their acceptability. The main reason for this was that it was considered that the health sector should focus on providing for better health not saving money. Even respondents with an economic background agreed that economic arguments were useful, but should always be accompanied by other types of arguments related to improving health or ensuring a better quality of life.

Explicitly stating the economic cost of ill-health or the savings made to the economy by preventing illness was also considered to be useful. Such costs have been calculated for the economic burden of road-traffic injuries, disability and mortality, as well as for the consequences of overweight and obesity.

Table 5 summarizes the economic arguments used in the five public policy cases analysed, the focus of the programmes, the key information for policy-making, and the economic theory behind those arguments.

According to most of the respondents and the public policy analysis, there is little evidence of the economic impact of intersectoral actions addressing SDH. Therefore, it is necessary to continue this line of research to obtain robust results on the impact of such actions. Currently, there is little available evidence assessing whether economic benefits have been achieved with the reviewed intersectoral actions, except for Oportunidades and Seguro Popular. Most of the evidence found showed impact results only in terms of population health *(37)*.

Finally, even if the best evidence were available, in terms of health, equity or economic impact, it would need to be translated into action. To achieve this, two elements are important according to one of the top government officials interviewed:

First, it requires that decision makers have a clear understanding that addressing social determinants will ultimately have an impact on health, and second ... an effective leadership that manages to enforce a shared intersectoral agenda based on strong empirical evidence.

Table 5. Economic arguments used for setting the social determinants of health agenda

Arguments used	Public policy	Programme focus	Key information for framing the issue in economic terms	Economic theory
Economic costs of obesity	ANSA	Health promotion strategies	• Direct costs (those associated with treating illness)	Efficiency-based
Economic costs of road injuries	IMESEVI	Safe-road promotion strategies	• Direct costs (those associated with treating illness) • Indirect costs (associated with loss of productivity due to morbidity or premature death)	Efficiency-based
Economic benefits of investing in human capital	PDHO	Development of basic capacities (health, nutrition, and education)	• Higher productivity • Higher labour supply • Improved skills as a result of greater education and training	Efficiency-based
Equality of opportunity on human capital			• Better health, improved nutrition and increased education have a synergistic effect that helps break the intergenerational poverty transmission	Equity-based
Economic costs of uninsurance	Seguro Popular	Financial protection	• Diminishing the risk of catastrophic health expenditures for vulnerable populations	Equity-based
Rural underdevelopment[1]	PDZP	Social development (health, education, housing, income, infrastructure, and ecological sustainability)	• Reducing the depth and severity of poverty and underdevelopment	Equity-based

1 Rural underdevelopment is largely determined by socioeconomic status, and is in turn a determinant of inter-generationally transmitted inequalities.

6 Lessons from Mexico

Overall, the analysis of the Mexican public policy cases shows that an intersectoral approach to address SDH is feasible, but difficult to implement for three main reasons. First, social factors are still not fully recognized as determinants of health by all policy- and decision-makers, including the medically biased health sector. The term itself is not well known. Second, shared budgets or at least resource allocation based on common goals are still awaiting a window of opportunity when the effective achievement of intersectoral alignment can be addressed. Finally, political barriers need to be overcome to improve intersectoral implementation. Political will and leadership at the highest level is key to achieving intersectoral actions addressing SDH. Furthermore, this intersectoral approach is more effective when it is followed from the beginning of the policy-making process, its planning phase.

Findings show that the design of intersectoral public polices has been based on strong empirical evidence. This has helped their incorporation into the agenda for implementation. However, formal and rigorous evaluations have not been conducted except for Oportunidades and Seguro Popular. The most recent public policies analysed, the Programme for the Development of Priority Zones, the Mexican Road Safety Initiative, and the National Agreement for Healthy Food have not been fully implemented and evaluated. When the need to evaluate arises, budgets tend to be targeted more often at implementing projects than to measuring their impact on health and other determinants.

Economic arguments such as the return on investment in recreational spaces for physical activities, estimating the cost-effectiveness of preventive measures, or measuring the financial protection effects of public insurance schemes, such as Seguro Popular, are necessary, but not sufficient to convince decision-makers both within and outside the health sector to design and implement public policies tackling SDH. Other arguments such as empirical evidence of the health benefits or the ethical value of health itself are also useful for pushing these public policies onto the agenda, particularly if there is very little information in economic or monetary terms to both assess and support these types of policies.

References and other resources

References

1. *Adelaide Statement on Health in All Policies.* World Health Organization, Government of South Australia, Adelaide 2010.

2. Commission on Social Determinants of Health. *Closing the gap in a generation: health equity through action on the social determinants of health. Final Report of the Commission on Social Determinants of Health.* Geneva, World Health Organization, 2008.

3. Starfield B. The Hidden Equity in Health Care. *International Journal for Equity in Health,* 2011, 10:15.

4. Largarde M, Haines A, Palmer N. *The impact of conditional cash transfers on health outcomes and use of health services in low and middle income countries.* Cochrane Database System Review 2009, 7:CD008137.

5. Knaul FM et al. The quest for universal health coverage: achieving social protection for all in Mexico. *The Lancet,* 2012, 380:1259–1279.

6. Gakidou E et al. Assessing the effect of the 2001-06 Mexican health reform: an interim report card. *The Lancet,* 2006, 368:1920–1935.

7. Hernández B et al. *Evaluación del impacto de Oportunidades en la mortalidad materna e infantil. En Resultados de la Evaluación Externa del Programa de Desarrollo Humano Oportunidades 2003.* Mexico City, Secretaría de Desarrollo Social, 2004.

8. Behrman J et al. *Evaluación de los efectos a diez años de Oportunidades en el desarrollo, educación y nutrición en niños entre 7 y 10 años de familias incorporadas desde el inicio del Programa. En Evaluación externa del Programa Oportunidades 2008. A diez años de intervención en zonas rurales (1997-2007) Tomo I. Efectos de Oportunidades en áreas rurales a diez años de intervención.* Mexico City, Secretaría de Desarrollo Social, 2008.

9. González de la Rocha M. *La vida después de Oportunidades: impacto del Programa a diez años de su creación. En Evaluación externa del Programa Oportunidades 2008. A diez años de intervención en zonas rurales (1997–2007) Tomo I. Efectos de Oportunidades en áreas rurales a diez años de intervención.* Mexico City, Secretaría de Desarrollo Social, 2008.

10. Gutiérrez JP et al. *Evaluación de la calidad de los servicios de atención a la salud asignados a la población beneficiaria de Oportunidades. En Evaluación externa del Programa Oportunidades 2008. A diez años de intervención en zonas rurales (1997–2007) Tomo I. Efectos de Oportunidades en áreas rurales a diez años de intervención.* Mexico City, Secretaría de Desarrollo Social, 2008.

11. *Health equity through intersectoral action: An analysis of 18 country case studies.* Geneva, World Health Organization / Public Health Agency of Canada, 2008.

12. Exworthy M. Policy to tackle the social determinants of health: using conceptual models to understand the policy process. *Health Policy and Planning*, 2008, 23:318–327.

13. Moresting F et al. *Method for synthesizing knowledge about public policies.* Quebec, National Collaborating Centre for Health Public Policy, 2011.

14. Chomik T. *Lessons learned from Canadian experiences with intersectoral action to address the social determinants of health.* Ottawa, Public Health Agency of Canada, 2007.

15. Jorgensen M. *Evaluating cross-sector partnerships.* Copenhagen, University of Aarhus, 2006.

16. Health Canada. *Intersectoral Action Toolkit.* Edmonton, Health Canada, 2000.

17. Kaleagonkar A, Brown LD. *Intersectoral cooperation: Lessons for practice.* Boston, Institute for Development Research, 2000 (IDR Report 16).

18. Levy S. *Progress against poverty: sustaining Mexico's PROGRESA-OPORTUNIDADES Program.* Washington, DC, Brookings Institution Press, 2006.

19. *Oportunidades: quince años de resultados. Coordinación Nacional del Programa de Desarrollo Humano Oportunidades,* Mexico City, Secretaría de Desarrollo, 2012.

20. Nadeau S et al. *Investing in young children: an early childhood development guide for policy dialogue and project preparation.* Washington, DC, The World Bank, 2011.

21. Frenk et al. *Fair financing and universal social protetection: the structural reform of the Mexican Health System.* Mexico City, Ministry of Health, 2004.

22. Secretaría de Salud. *Financiamiento justo y protección social universal: La Reforma Estructural del Sistema de Salud en México.* Mexico City, 2004.

23. Frenk J et al. Comprehensive reform to improve health system performance in Mexico. *The Lancet*, 2006, 368:1524–1534.

24. Ortiz M. El Seguro Popular: Una crónica de la democracia mexicana. Mexico City, Fondo de Cultura Económica, 2006.

25. Knaul F et al. 2012. The quest for universal health coverage: achieving social protection for all in Mexico. *The Lancet*, 2012, 380:1259–1279.

26. Pan American Health Organization. *IMESEVI: la Iniciativa Mexicana de Seguridad Vial.* Washington, DC, 2012 (https://new.paho.org/mex/index.php?option=com_content&task=view&id=491&Itemid=375, accessed 23 March 2013).

27. Hijar M et al. Quantifying the underestimated burden of road traffic mortality in Mexico: A comparison of three approaches. *Traffic Injury Prevention*, 2012, 13(Suppl.):5–10.

28. Centro Nacional de Prevención de Accidentes. *Iniciativa Mexicana de Seguridad Vial y Prevención de Lesiones en el Tránsito (IMESEVI). Construcción de Línea Base. Reporte final.* 1a ed. Mexico City, Secretaría de Salud, 2009.

29. Gobierno Federal. *Plan Nacional de Desarrollo,* 2007–2012. Mexico City, 2007.

30. *Acuerdo mediante el cual se establecen los lineamientos generales para el expendio o distribución de alimentos y bebidas en los establecimientos de consumo escolar de los planteles de educación básica. Lunes 23 de agosto.* Mexico City, Diario Oficial de la Federación, 2010.

31. Gutiérrez JP et al. *Encuesta Nacional de Salud y Nutrición 2012. Resultados Nacionales.* Cuernavaca, Instituto Nacional de Salud Pública, 2012.

32. Secretaría de Salud. *Estrategia 100x100: componente de salud. Programa de Acción Específico 2008-2012.* Mexico City, Secretaría de Salud, 2008.

33. Secretaría de Salud. *Acuerdo Nacional para la Salud Alimentaria. Estrategia contra el sobrepeso y la obesidad.* Mexico City, 2010.

34. Rivera J et al. *Asesoría para realizar un estudio cuantitativo sobre la aplicación de la segunda etapa de los lineamientos generales para el expendio o distribución de alimentos y bebidas en los establecimientos de consumo escolar de los planteles de educación básica.* Cuernavaca, Centro de Investigación en Nutrición y Salud, Instituto Nacional de Salud Pública, 2012.

35. Mayer D. The long-term impact of health on economic growth in Mexico, 1950-1995. *Journal of International Development,* 2001, 13:123–126.

36. Comisión Mexicana sobre Macroeconomía y Salud. *Macroeconomía y salud. Invertir en salud para el desarrollo económico.* Mexico City, Fondo de Cultura Económica, 2006.

37. Figueroa A. *Documento de posicionamiento sobre argumento económicos de acciones intersectoriales que fortalecen los Determinantes Sociales de la Salud.* Documento para discusión. Mexico City, Pan American Health Organization, 2012.

Other information resources

Atun R et al. A systematic review of the evidence on integration of targeted health invderventions into health systems. *Health Policy and Planning,* 2010, 25:1–14.

Barquera S et al. *Bases técnicas del Acuerdo Nacional para la Salud Alimentaria. Estrategia contra el sobrepeso y la obesidad.* Mexico City, Secretaría de Salud, 2010.

Brown L et al. *Cost of inaction on the social determinants of health.* Canberra, National Centre for Social and Economic Modelling, 2012.

Coordinación Nacional del Programa de Desarrollo Humano Oportunidades. *Plan Estratégico de Mediano Plazo, 2007-2012.* Mexico City, Secretaría de Desarrollo Social, 2008.

Cordera R y Murayama C (Coordinadores). *Los determinantes sociales de la salud en México.* Mexico City, Fondo de Cultura Económica, 2012.

Evci-Kiraz ED et al. Local decision makers' awareness of the social determinants of health in Turkey: a cross-sectional study. *BMC Public Health,* 2012, 12:437.

Fizbein A, Schady N. *Conditional cash transfers. Reducing present and future poverty.* Washington, DC, World Bank, 2009.

Graham H. Tackling inequalities in health in England: remedying health disadvantages, narrowing health gaps or reducing health gradients? *Journal of Social Policy,* 2004, 33:115–151.

Lavin T, Metcalfe O. *Economic arguments for addressing social determinants of health inequalities.* Brussels, DETERMINE: an EU consortium for Action on the Socioeconomic Determinants of Health, 2009.

Levy S. *Good intentions, bad outcomes: Social policy, informality and economic growth in Mexico.* Washington, DC, Brookings Institution Press, 2008.

Marmot M. Social determinants of health inequalities. *The Lancet*, 2005, 365:1099–1104.

Martínez Valle A. Social class, marginality and self-assessed health: a cross-sectional analysis of the health gradient in Mexico. *International Journal for Equity in Health*, 2009, 8:3.

Ministry of Health and Social Policy. *Moving forward equity in health: monitoring social determinants of health and the reduction of health inequalities.* Madrid, 2010.

Muntaner C, Ng E, Chung H. *Better Health: An analysis of public policy and programming focusing on the determinants of health and health outcomes that are effective in achieving the healthiest populations.* Ottawa, ON, Canadian Health Services Research Foundation, 2012.

Ministry of Health and Care Services. *National strategy to reduce social inequalities in health.* Oslo, 2007.

World Health Organization. *Declaración política de Río sobre determinantes sociales de la salud. 21 de octubre de 2011.* Rio de Janeiro, 2011.

World Health Organization. *World Conference on Social Determinants of Health: Closing the Gap: Policy into Practice on Social Determinants of Health.* Rio de Janeiro, 2011.

National Collaborating Centre for Determinants of Health. *Assessing the impact and effectiveness of intersectoral action on the social determinants of health and health equity: An expedited systematic review.* Antigonish, NCCDH, St. Francis Xavier University, 2012.

Rohregger B. *Social determinants of health: The role of social protection in addressing social inequalities in health.* Eschborn, Gesellschaft für Internationale Zusammenarbeit, 2011 (Discussion Paper 11).

Secretaría de Desarrollo Social. *Reglas de Operación del Programa para el Desarrollo de Zonas Prioritarias 2011.* Mexico City, SEDESOL, 2010.

Secretaría de Salud. *Programa Nacional de Salud. Por un México sano: construyendo alianzas para una mejor salud.* Mexico City, 2007.

Solar O, Irwin A. *A conceptual framework for action on the social determinants of health.* Geneva, Comission on Social Determinants of Health, World Health Organization, 2007.

Suhrcke M et al. *Chronic disease: An economic perspective.* London, Oxford Health Alliance, 2006.

World Health Organization. *Intersectoral action to tackle the social determinants of health and the role of evaluation. Report of the 1st Meeting of the WHO Policy Maker Resource Group on Social Determinants of Health, Viña del Mar, 27–29 January, 2010.* Geneva, 2010.

World Health Organization. *Report of a Conference on Intersectoral Action for Health.* Halifax, Nova Scotia, 20-23 April 1997. Geneva, 1997.

Appendix

Appendix 1. Profile of respondents

Number	Current institution	Criteria for selection
1	National Council for Evaluation of Social Policies	Regulates most federal public policy evaluations
2	Independent consultant	Major role in the design and implementation of the programme for the Development of Priority Zones.
3	National Coordination of Oportunidades Program	Major role in the design and implementation of the Oportunidades Program for Human Development.
4	National Academy of Medicine	Coordinates the Social Determinants of Health Comission of the National Academy of Medicine and was Deputy Minister of Health.
5	Ministry of Health	Current Deputy Minister of Health for Health Prevention and Promotion
6	National Women's Institute	Major role in the planning and evaluation of gender public policies
7	Research Institute for Economic Development	Senior economist on inequality and poverty
8	National Comission for Social Protection on Health	Major role in the design and implementation of health-care policies
9	Mexican Institute for Social Security	Senior economist and coordinator of the Mexican Commission on Macroeconomics and Health
10	Harvard Kennedy School of Government	Major role in the evaluation of public policies designed and implemented by the Ministry of Social Development
11	Inter-American Development Bank	Senior economist on social protection
12	National Institute of Public Health	Senior medical researcher on nutrition and public policy evaluation
13	National Institute of Public Health	Senior medical researcher on global health and social determinants of health

Appendix 2. Questionnaire[1]

Good morning (afternoon). I am doing research as an independent consultant for the World Health Organization. The purpose of this study is to know your opinion about the design and implementation of public policies that influence the social determinants of health. For purposes of the study, your responses will remain anonymous. May I ask you the following questions? The interview should last approximately 45 minutes.

Knowledge of the determinants of health

1. Do you know or are familiar with the social determinants of health?

If the answer is negative go to number 2 and read out. If yes skip to question 3.

2. Health is determined by many factors, which are outside the scope of the health sector. The term social determinants of health (SOCIAL DETERMINANTS OF HEALTH) is generally used to focus on the social conditions in which people live and which affect their health, such as income, schooling or access to drinking water.

3. From your perspective, do you consider that public policies are formulated to improve those social conditions that affect the health of people in Mexico? Could you identify some of them?

If the response is negative go to question 4. If yes, skip to question 5.

4. If it is not the case, why do you consider public policies with this approach are not formulated?

5. Have issues related to social health determinants been discussed within your sector?

6. Would you be willing to collaborate with the health sector or other sectors to achieve health goals?

7. What kind of actions have you taken or could take within your sector to influence social health determinants?

8. Do you consider that there is enough commitment or political will to achieve them?

9. Do you consider that these identified public policies have had an impact on improving health?

10. Could you identify empirical evidence to sustain this argument?

---

[1] The content of this questionnaire was modified according to the profile and experience of the respondent. For example, knowledge of the health sector questions were only asked to those outside that sector.

Experience and capacity for intersectoral cooperation

11. Recently it has been argued that these policies would be more effective if they were implemented intersectorally, i.e. with the joint participation of various government agencies.

In your professional experience (specify when and where) have you ever conducted any kind of cooperation with other public sectors?

12. What factors have contributed to achieving this cooperation?

13. What were the main challenges?

Knowledge of the health sector

14. Is health a relevant issue for your sector?

15. Do you take into account the impact of your sector on public health?

16. If the health sector or some other sector invited you to collaborate in any programme or policy to influence the SOCIAL DETERMINANTS OF HEALTH, what would be the main obstacles to effective cooperation?

Evidence for decision-making

17. Information is useful to support the formulation and implementation of public policy. What information would be most helpful in your sector to support effective actions for collaboration with the health sector? (Evidence to define a problem of public health, best practices, policy priorities.)

18. Do you know any impact evaluations conducted in your sector? Would you be willing to be evaluated on the health impact of your public policies?

19. How could the health sector support your sector in addressing the social determinants of health?

Economic arguments

20. Do you know of any initiatives or efforts to analyse the health impacts of these public policies aimed at addressing the social determinants of health in economic terms? Please provide as many possible examples as you can identify.

21. Are economic arguments used to support these policies? Please cite examples of how these arguments are articulated. If the response is negative skip to question 23. If yes, go to question 22.

22. Which government or nongovernmental organization units make these arguments?
To whom are these arguments made?

23. If economic arguments are not used to justify these public policies, please explain why you think they are not used.

24. What economic arguments do you consider would help align your interests with those of the health sector in order to participate in a joint initiative to improve the health of the population?

Notes

Notes